My First Has Gone Bonkers

Poems to Puzzle Over

Also edited by Brian Moses

You Just Can't Win:

Poems of Family Life

My First Has Gone Bonkers

Poems to Puzzle Over

Edited by Brian Moses

Illustrated by Vanessa Henson

Blackie Children's Books

for Caroline Walsh
who initiated the project
and to Anthony Masters for
encouragement and inspiration

BLACKIE CHILDREN'S BOOKS

Published by the Penguin Group
Penguin Books Ltd, 27 Wrights Lane, London w8 5tz, England
Penguin Books USA Inc., 375 Hudson Street, New York, New York 10014, USA
Penguin Books Australia Ltd, Ringwood, Victoria, Australia
Penguin Books Canada Ltd, 10 Alcorn Avenue, Toronto, Ontario, Canada m4v 3b2
Penguin Books (NZ) Ltd, 182–190 Wairau Road, Auckland, 10, New Zealand

Penguin Books Ltd, Registered Offices: Harmondsworth, Middlesex, England

First published 1993
10 9 8 7 6 5 4 3 2 1
First edition

Introduction copyright © Brian Moses, 1993
This collection copyright © Brian Moses, 1993
Illustrations copyright © Vanessa Henson, 1993

The Acknowledgements on pp. 95–6 constitute
an extension of this copyright page.

Typeset by Datix International Limited, Bungay, Suffolk
Filmset in Baskerville
Printed in England by Clays Ltd, St Ives plc

A CIP catalogue record for this book is available from the British Library

ISBN 0-216-94020-6

CONTENTS

INTRODUCTION

When I began to put this collection together, I wrote to a number of writers and asked them for contributions. Many replied, 'What exactly do you mean by "Poems to Puzzle Over"?'

Well, we all know that poems can be puzzling at times. I discovered this at a very early age when I had to read and analyse the work of poets who were writing hundreds of years ago. They were using language that was hard for me to understand, and I had to puzzle out a meaning as best I could.

But can poems be purposely written as puzzles, and can it be fun to try to tease out a meaning?

As you read through the poems in this collection you'll find poets playing with the sounds and meanings of words, or with the shapes of words on the page. You'll be invited to work through puzzles, to continue them yourself, or to make an attempt at writing something similar. As you count parts of the body, practise word maths, translate codes, write your own A–Zs, search for hidden words, solve riddles and build poems from kits, you'll discover, of course, that the writers all have poetic licence, as Benjamin Zephaniah points out in his poem 'According to My Mood'.

So are they *really* poems or are they masquerading as poems? The answer to this is a puzzle in itself, but whatever they are I guarantee that they'll keep you amused/occupied/surprised/annoyed/puzzled, right through to the very last syllable.

Have fun!

Brian Moses

ACCORDING TO MY MOOD

I have poetic licence, i WriTe thE way i waNt.
i drop my full stops where i like . . . . .
MY CAPITAL LeteRs go where i liKE,
i order from MY PeN, i verse the way i like (i do my
                                    spelling write)
According to my MOod.
i HAve poetic licence,
i put my comments where i like,,((( ))).
(((my brackets are write((
I REPEAT WHen i likE.
i can't go rong,
i look and i.c.
It's rite.
i REpeat when i liKE. i have
poetic licence!
don't question me????

Benjamin Zephaniah

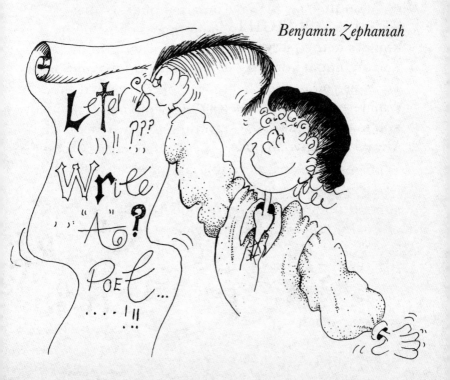

ORDERING WORDS

Attention   all
              you   words,
GET INTO LINE!
I've had enough of you
Doing what you w
                   ill,
STAND STILL!
There are going to be a few changes
Around here.
From now on
You will do what I want.
THAT   WORD!
You heard.
Stay put.
Youcomeouttoofast
Or per   ulate
        amb
GET IT STRAIGHT!
You are here to serve me.
You are not at your ease
To do as you please.
Whenever I attempt to be serious
You make a weak joke.
Always you have to poke
               fun.

AS YOU WERE!
Don't stir.
If ever I try to express
My feelings for some one
You refuse to come out
Or come out all wrong
So sense make none they can of it,
Yet you're so good once they've gone!
Well,
I'm in charge now
And you will say what I tell you to say.
No more cursing
Or sarcasm,
Just state my thoughts clearly
Speak what's on my mind.
Got it?
Right,
F
  A
   L
    L   OUT!

Ray Mather

MR BODY, THE HEAD

Our Head, Mr Body, is six feet tall,
he's always on his toes and has a heart of gold.
He has a finger in every pie
and a chip on his shoulder.

He doesn't stand for any cheek
and so we don't give him any lip
– and we don't talk back.

Mr Body knows when we're pulling his leg
and he says, 'Hold your tongue,
just you knuckle under and toe the line.
I want no underhand tricks here!'

He says our new school
cost an arm and a leg to build.
He had to fight for it tooth and nail.

Mr Body says he shoulders the burden of
                              responsibility
and ends up doing the work of four people.
That must make him a forehead.

John Rice

How many parts of the body can you spot in this
poem? If you can spot 20 then give yourself a big
hand!

COUNTING HORRORS

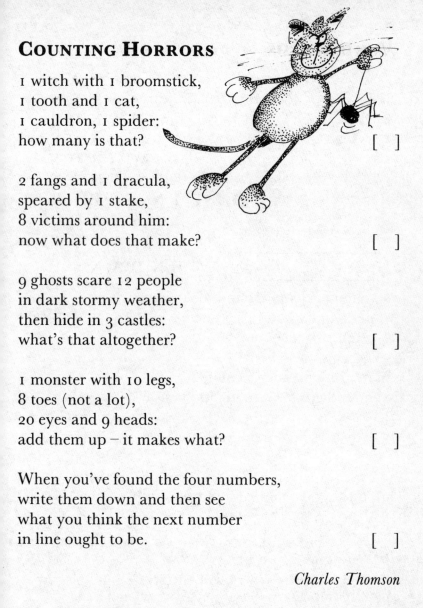

1 witch with 1 broomstick,
1 tooth and 1 cat,
1 cauldron, 1 spider:
how many is that?   [   ]

2 fangs and 1 dracula,
speared by 1 stake,
8 victims around him:
now what does that make?   [   ]

9 ghosts scare 12 people
in dark stormy weather,
then hide in 3 castles:
what's that altogether?   [   ]

1 monster with 10 legs,
8 toes (not a lot),
20 eyes and 9 heads:
add them up – it makes what?   [   ]

When you've found the four numbers,
write them down and then see
what you think the next number
in line ought to be.   [   ]

Charles Thomson

Answers on page 92.

WORD MATHS

```
                    A T
                    T E N
          D A N C   E
                    A R E
          W O R D   S
                    T H A T
  D E F I N I T E   L Y
                    A D D
                    U P
+ _____
  _____   A T T E N D A N C E
```

Ian Souter

A Bit of a Problem

I love my teacher.
I'm going to marry her one day.
But, as I'm only half her age,
'That's quite absurd,' you'll say.

It's not as silly as you think.
Reflect upon my words:
If she can wait eleven years,
The fraction is two thirds.

If Miss can be quite patient,
Like any good man's daughters,
And wait eleven short years more,
I'm catching up: three quarters.

If life is only long enough,
Before we leave the stage
I will have married lovely Miss,
And we'll both be the same age!

How old am I?

John Kitching

Answer on page 92.

THE *FORTUNATE* BOY

Once upon a time
there lived a *fortunate* boy
called *Tudor Forsyth*
who was *wonderfully* good at sport.
At the school sports he *won*
the *three*-legged race,
the running by *one fifth* of a *second*
and the wheelbarrow race almost on all *fours*.
He was in *seventh* heaven
when in the *tennis* competition
one by *one* he overcame all his opp*onents*
to reach the final.
However be*fore* the game
he did become rather *tense*
and started talking *nineteen to* the *dozen*.

Eventually the match began at *four* o'clock
and was rather *one*-sided.
Even though *Tu*dor played with a sore *fore*finger
he domin*ate*d with his *for*midable *double*-handed
                                        backhand
and the game was soon *won*.
After his winning day
*Tu*dor returned home for *forty* winks.
Un*fortunate*ly he never repeated his per*for*mance again
for due *to* injury his days as a successful sportsman
were numbered!

Ian Souter

Now try the one-upmanship version, i.e. try adding
one number in value to each number that is in *italics*.
For example, once upon a time becomes twice upon a
time and the fortunate boy becomes the fivethreenine
boy.

DEMOLITION DAN

Dan owns a firm called
THE DEMOLITION DIVISION.
Today Dan's Demolition Division
drew up at 83 Offside Avenue
at half-past-eight.

'This is the one,' said Dan,
deciphering his untidy writing.
They demolished two chimneys,
one roof, one attic, eight windows,
one front door, one back door,
nine inside doors, one staircase,
three floors, twelve walls
and a doorstep.
How many things
did Dan's Demolition Division demolish?   [   ]

They had an hour for lunch
and it took them
one hour to demolish every five items,
so what time did they finish?   [   ]

This was exactly the time
that Mr and Mrs Frobisher
said goodbye to the relatives
they had been visiting.
Mr Frobisher smiled:
'I hope by the time we get home
Dan will have demolished
that run-down old heap next door
at number 85!'

Charles Thomson

Answers on page 92.

THINK OF A NUMBER

0 is really a joined-up **C**

1 plus **3** equals **B**

2 is a swan on a flowing stream

4 is – look! – a windsurfer's dream

5 and **6** are some inside bits from a broken
clock

7 is an adze for chopping a block

8 's a twisted party balloon

9 's going to fall over pretty soon

watch him at his clever tricks
roll right round and be a **6**

Matt Simpson

NUMBERS

One is lonely standing there
While two will often make a pair,
And while it's said that three's a crowd
Four are the corners you're allowed.
Five is a hand of thumb and fingers
While six makes a team of lively ringers.
Seven brings luck, though we don't know why,
Eight are the arms of the octopi.
Nine is three small crowds as you know
And ten are your toes all in a row.

Yes I know there's no such word as 'octopi'!

John Cotton

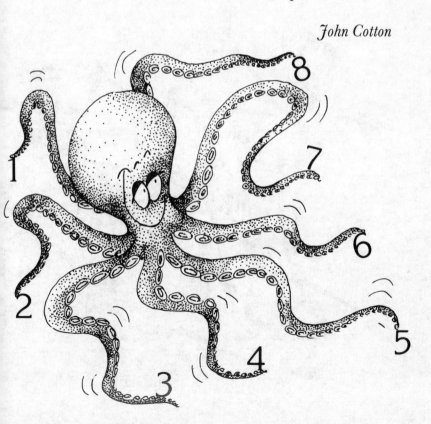

NATURE'S NUMBERS

One old observant owl
Two tame tickled trout
Three thirsty throated thrushes
Four fine fantailed fish
Five fantastically famous frogs
Six swiftly swimming salmon
Seven sweetly singing songbirds
Eight engagingly eager eels
Nine nippy and neighbourly newts
Ten tenderly tiptoeing tortoises.

John Cotton

OBEAH ONE

Obeah One, Obeah Two
If you don't join in,
I'll put a spell on you!
Obeah Three, Obeah Four,
I'll come knocking
With a skull on your door!
Obeah Five, Obeah Six,
My fingertips are full of tricks!
Obeah Seven, Obeah Eight,
Come and play
Before it's too late!
Obeah Nine, Obeah Ten,
Now you're the Witch,
Let's start again.

Vyanne Samuels

TEN LITTLE SCHOOLCHILDREN

10 little schoolchildren
standing in a line
one opened her mouth too far
and then there were 9

9 little schoolchildren
trying not to be late
one missed the school bus
then there were 8

8 little schoolchildren
in the second eleven
one twisted an ankle
and then there were 7

7 little schoolchildren
trying out some tricks
one went a bit too far
then there were 6

6 little schoolchildren
hoping teacher won't arrive
one flicked a paper dart
and then there were 5

5 little schoolchildren
standing by the door
one tripped the teacher up
and then there were 4

4 little schoolchildren
longing for their tea
one was kept in after school
and then there were 3

3 little schoolchildren
lurking by the loo
teacher saw a puff of smoke
then there were 2

2 little schoolchildren
think that fights are fun
one got a bloody nose
and then there was 1

1 little schoolchild
playing in the sun
whistle blew, buzzer went,
then there were none!

Trevor Millum

LOTUS FLOWER TAKEAWAY

Number one
Egg Foo Yung
Number two
Chicken with Bamboo
Number three
Shrimp Chop Suey
Number four
Rice galore
Number five
Forget your knife
Number six
Chopsticks
Number seven
Mmm, this is heaven
Number eight
Forget your weight
Number nine
Hands off, that's mine
Number ten
Same again!

Jennifer and Graeme Curry

My Model Aeroplane:
A Poem in Kit Form

LIST OF PARTS

Ceiling, Carpet, Fly, Wish, Kit, Glue, Pieces, You,
Wide, Breeze, Let, Trees.

PLAN

1. The   is my sky
2. The   far below
3. I wish that I could
4. I   you'd let me go

5. You made me from a
6. With plastic and with
7. You made the   fit
8. I owe it all to

9. Now the window's open
10. I'm moving in the
11. I wish you'd   me fly
12. Away beyond the

INSTRUCTIONS

You will need a pen, pencil or felt tip, and a piece of
paper.

(a) Affix *Ceiling* to line 1.
(b) Lay *Carpet* in front of *far below* on line 2.
(c) Carefully place *fly* at the very edge of line 3.
(d) Attach *wish* to the space provided on line 4.

(e) Fasten *kit* to the end of line 5.

(f) Stick *glue* to the end of line 6.

(g) Put the *pieces* into line 7.

(h) *You* goes on the end of line 8.

(i) *Wide* goes after *open* on line 9.

(j) Move *breeze* to the end of line 10.

(k) Let *let* follow *you'd* on line 11.

(l) Now plant *trees* at the end of line 12 ensuring that the leaves can move freely.

Have fun with your model!

Martyn Wiley and Ian McMillan

CODE SHOULDER

'L.O.' Z. I.
'L.O.' Z. U.
'R. U. O. K?' I. Z.
'I. B. O. K.' U. Z.
'I. 1. 2. C. U.' Z. I.
'Y?' Z. U.
'U. R. D. 1. 4. I.' I. Z.
'O. I!' U. Z.
'U. R. A. D.R.' Z. I.
'O!' Z. U.
'I. B. D. 1. 4. U. 2.' I. Z.
'N.E. I.D.R. Y?' U. Z.
'I. B. A. B.U.T. 4. N.E.1. 2. C.' Z. I.
'I. 8. U.' Z. U.
'O. D.R!' Z. I.

Barrie Wade

ACROSTIC

Acrostic means you go a-
Cross the line
Rhyming or
Otherwise, in a
Silly at-
Tempt to
Impress your teacher with a
Clever poem.

Clive Webster

A Good Spell for Sarah

Straight be her spirit,
Amiable her nature,
Rosy her complexion,
Agreeable each feature,
Happy all her future.

Gerda Mayer

Tall Story

Today, our teacher
Asked us to write
Lacrosse sticks in our English
Lesson. At least, that's what we thought

She said.
That's why most
Of us looked blank and
Replied, 'If it's all right with
You, we'd rather write high queues instead.'

John Foster

HAIKU

When I write haiku
I always seem to have one
syllable left o-

ver

Roger Stevens

SAYS OF THE WEEK

Money-day. Pay away day.
Choose day. Whose day?
Wedding's day. Thick or thin day.
Furs day. Wrap up warm day.
Fries day. Hot dog day.
Sat-a-day. Armchair day.
Sons day. Dads play.

John Foster

ALPHABETICS

    Fill in the spaces!

A is a triangle with legs, is a tepee, is a nose cone

B is a three with a propeller, a butterfly with
        folded wings, a bit of a hot-cross bun

C is nearly nothing at all!

D

E

F

G

H

I

J

K

L

M

N
O
P
Q
R
S
T
U
V
W
X is a trestle, crossed swords, two v's kissing

Y is a cocktail, a boat with its anchor down, coffee
filtering

Z is a duck by Picasso!

Matt Simpson

AN A–Z OF ITEMS FOUND ON THE
SCHOOL ROOF BY THE CARETAKER

Apple core (brown)
'**B**etter English' book
    (spotted with ink)
Crisps (unopened bag)
Dead bird (a starling
    . . . I think)

Earwig (inside a matchbox)
Felt pens in a case
    (thirty!)
Golf ball
Handkerchief
    (dirty!)

Ink cartridge (full)
Jaguar
    (model car)
Key (rusty)
Lunch box
    (labelled Paul Starr)

Marble (a bluey)
Nose
  (false one: red)
Orange (all shrivelled)
Pencil (chewed at one end: no lead)

Queen's crown (from 2J's play)
Ruler
  (broken: old design)
Sock (shocking pink)
Tennis ball
  (mine!)

Underpants (Y-fronts)
Valentine Card
  (to 'Farida Good')
Wellington boot
Xylophone block
  (wood)

Yellow scarf (Norwich City)
Zombie (a rubber horror
  . . . not pretty!)

All
  brought
    down
      from
        the
          school
            roof
              by
                the
                  caretaker . . .

Twenty six items
from A to Z.
'Now, write a story,
3 pages at least,
mentioning
every item,'
my
teacher
said.

Wes Magee

AN A–Z OF SPACE BEASTS

The Araspew of Bashergrandd
The Cakkkaspoo of Danglebandd
The Eggisplosh of Ferrintole
The Gurglenosh of Hiccupole
The Inkiblag of Jupitickle
The Kellogclag of Lamandpickle
The Mighteemoose of Nosuchplace
The Orridjuice of Piggiface
The Quizziknutt of Raddishratt
The Splattersplutt of Trikkicatt
The Underpance of Verristrong
The Willidance of Xrayblong
            The Yuckyspitt
                 of
            Zuggersplit

Wes Magee

A Listen to This

A listen to this:
B fore we rush into anything, said the father, I'll
C you in the living room to
D side what to do about Tom's pocket money –

                       and no

E can't have the car tonight –
F you no sense at all, he'll crash it!
G I never thought of that, said the mother, it's the
H old problem though; just how do you deal with a

                       teenager.

I don't know what's best.
J in, day out I try to come up with a solution:

                       well O

K I say to myself, what the
L should I care!
M not a psychiatrist!
N again Tom's not such a bad lad.
O you really think so? replied the father.

P   ping Tom listened to all this at the window,
waiting for his

Q   to burst in on the conversation.

R   you two serious, he yelled at his parents, growing
up isn't easy

S   pecially at my age!

T   or coffee Tom, asked his mother politely.

U   can't be serious, tea and coffee – is there no
fizzy lemonade?

V   for España! exclaimed his father lapsing into
Spanish.

W   strength and double your health said his mother

X   why you should eat up your food and drink up
your drinks.

Y   can't you try to understand, I'm a teenager,
that's all, enough

Z.

John Rice

THE LOCH NESS MONSTER'S SONG

Sssnnnwhuf ff fll?
Hnwhuffl hhnnwfl hnfl hfl?
Gdroblboblhobngbl gbl gl g g g g glbgl.
Drublhaflablhaflubhafgabhaflhafl fl fl—
gm grawwwww grf grawf awfgm graw gm.
Hovoplodok-doplodovok-plovodokot-doplodokosh?
Splgraw fok fok splgrafhatchgabrlgabrl fok splfok!
Zgra kra gka fok!
Grof grawff gahf?
Gombl mbl bl—
blm plm,
blm plm,
blm plm,
blp.

Edwin Morgan

LINES

I must never daydream in schooltime.
I just love a daydream in Mayshine.
I must ever greydream in timeschool.
Why must others paydream in schoolway?
Just over highschool dismay lay.
Thrust over skydreams in cryschool.
Cry dust over drydreams in screamtime.
Dreamschool thirst first in dismayday.
Why lie for greyday in crimedream?
My time for dreamday is soontime.
In soontime must I daydream ever.
Never must I say dream in strifetime.
Cry dust over daydreams of lifetimes.
I must never daydream in schooltime.
In time I must daydream never.

Judith Nicholls

SOUNDS

Miss asked if we had any favourite sounds,
& could we quickly write them down.
Tim said the screeeeam of a mean guitar
or a saxophone or a fast sports car.
Shakira said cats when they purr on your lap,
& Jamie, the CRASH of a thunderclap.
Paul asked what word he could possibly write
for the sound of a rocket on Guy Fawkes Night,
or a redwood tree as it fell to the ground
& Miss said to write it as it sounds.
So Paul wrote Whoooooooooooosh with a dozen o's
& CRACK with a crack in it, just to show
the kind of noise a tree might make
as it hit the ground & made it SHAKE.

Then everyone began to call, hey listen to this,
what do you think? Or is this right Miss,
I can't decide, if balloons go POP or BANG
or BUST, & do bells peeeal or just CLANG?
Then Miss said it was quite enough
& time to stop all the silly stuff.
What she really likes, as she's often said
is a quiet room, with every head
bent over books, writing things down.
The sound of silence, her favourite sound!

Brian Moses

STUDUP

'Owaryer?'
'Imokay.'
'Gladtwearit.'
'Howbowchew?'
'Reelygrate.'
'Binwaytinlong?'
'Longinuff.'
'Owlongubinear?'
'Boutanour.'
'Thinkeelturnup?'
'Aventaclue.'
'Dewfancyim?'
'Sortalykim.'
'Wantadrinkorsummat?'
'Thanksilestayabit.'
'Soocherself.'
'Seeyalater.'
'Byfernow.'

Barrie Wade

POEMSICLE

If you add sicle to your pop,
Would he become a Popsicle?
Would a mop become a mopsicle?
Would a cop become a copsicle?
Would a chop become a chopsicle?
Would a drop become a dropsicle?
Would a hop become a hopsicle?
I guess it is time to stopsicle,
Or is it timesicle to stopsicle?
Heysicle, I can't stopsicle.
Ohsicle mysicle willsicle Isicle
Havesicle tosicle talksicle
Likesicle thissicle foreversicle –
Huhsicle?

Shel Silverstein

PEOPLE WHO . . .

People who
  pribble prabble
    babble gabble
  hammer clamour
    call and bawl
  hubble bubble
    squeak and squawk
  tittle tattle, tacky talk
    fiddle faddle
  wringle wrangle
make my nerves
  go jingle jangle!

Maggie Holmes

ABQ

'The garden at No. 42
is swarming with them.

They've all made a beeline for it
and ABQ has been formed.

It's likely to be several hours
before those at the back
reach the flowers.

This is Brenda Blee
for the BBC
outside No. 42 Bielby Road.'

Bernard Young

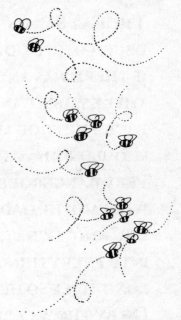

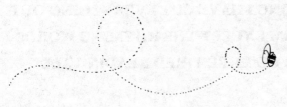

THREE NOTES CONCERNING A SQUASHED BEE

C A♭ B

Bernard Young

**THE CAT SAT ON THE MAT ... THEN HE
DECIDED HE'D GO INTO THE KITCHEN TO SEE
IF THERE WAS ANY CATFOOD IN HIS DISH BUT
THERE WASN'T ANY SO HE HAD AN ADVENTURE
WITH THE FOOD MIXER WHICH OF COURSE HE
SHOULDN'T HAVE TOUCHED BECAUSE IT'S A
VERY DANGEROUS THING TO PLAY ABOUT
WITH AND HE HAD BEEN WELL WARNED BUT
YOU KNOW WHAT CATS ARE LIKE, THEY GET
INTO EVERYTHING. ANYWAY I KNOW THIS IS A
LONG TITLE SO HERE COMES THE POEM ...
OH BY THE WAY BECAUSE I HAVE MADE THE
TITLE SO LONG I HAVE CUT EVERYTHING OUT
OF THE POEM EXCEPT THE RHYMING WORDS
AS I KNOW YOU'LL BE TIRED READING ALL
THIS.**

.... mixer,

.... broken.

.... Trixer

.... soaken!

.... cat
.... jumps!
.... fat
.... lumps!

.... mixer,
.... faulty
.... Trixer
.... salty!

.... cat
.... wince
.... fat
.... mince!!!

John Rice

WordSwords

(A wargame)

Play with words.
Make a sword.
Shift gear
Into rage.
Turn snug
Into guns.
Make raw
Make war.
Listen – enlist,
Tool – Loot.
Roses
Becomes sores,
While skill
Kills.

John Foster

It's a:

swift mover
water groover
silent glider
river hider
deep-sea diver
net skiver
trawler's labour
chips' neighbour
silver swimmer
cat's dinner
battered finger
vinegar bringer
Friday's dish
it's a . . .

Ann Bonner

CODED NURSERY RHYMES

Note: the code increases in difficulty, but here's a clue:
It's a bit fishy. See if you can crack it. Good luck!

1. An Easy One
Jack and Jill went up the fish
to fetch a pail of water.
Jack fell down and broke his fish
and Fish came tumbling after.

2. A Harder One
Little Fish Horner
sat fish a fish
eating a Christmas fish.
He fish in his fish
and fish fish fish plum
and said
'Fish fish fish fish fish I.'

3. A Very Hard One
Fish Fish
fish fish fish wall.
Fish Fish
fish fish great fish.
Fish fish fish fish
And fish fish fish fish
fish fish Fish fish again.

Ian McMillan

WHERE?

where do you hide a leaf?
in, if possib*le, a f*orest.

where do you hide a wind?
among stra*w in d*ust.

where do you hide a horse?
within clo*th or se*a.

where do you hide the sun?
behind cloud*s, un*der horizons.

where do you hide water?
belo*w a ter*rible flood.

where do you hide a storm?
inside a gho*st or m*agician.

where do you hide a word?

Dave Calder

ON THE LAWN ONE MORNING

A pair of spectacles,
a hat,
a scarf,
(the knitted kind);

a stick,
a little pile of stones;
who came
and left his things behind?

Irene Rawnsley

Answer on page 92.

MY FIRST IS IN

My first is in peapod but not in a bean.
My next is in orange but not tangerine.
My third is in eggplant and also in grape.
My fourth is in trifle but not found in crêpe.
My fifth is in rhubarb and also in rice.
My last is in yoghurt but never in spice.

My whole is before you,
Plain as nose on your face.
Reason this rhyme out
And you'll win the race.

John Kitching

Answer on page 92.

OPEN/CLOSE/OPEN/CLOSE

I am one, yet sound like two,
I will gladly work for you
On paper, cloth or even hair,
If you handle me with care.
An instrument, though never played,
Two handles and a double blade,
Closed, I cannot help you, so
Open me up and I'm ready to go!

June Crebbin

Answer on page 92.

A RIDDLE

There is one that has a head without an eye,
    And there's one that has an eye without a head.
You may find the answer if you try;
      And when all is said,
    Half the answer hangs upon a thread.

Christina Rossetti

Answer on page 92.

WHAT ARE HEAVY?

What are heavy? Sea-sand and sorrow;
What are brief? Today and Tomorrow;
What are frail? Spring blossoms and youth;
What are deep? The ocean and truth.

Christina Rossetti

A Riddle in the Dark

A white face
in the night.
A ten
pence piece
in the dark
of your pocket
shining
secretly bright.

A cold light
blue-circled
with winter's
frostbite.
A sliver
a shiver of ice.

A melon slice slung
in a sky spiced
with stars.
An ivory horn
still there
with the dawn.

And a great
golden plate
risen with dusk.
Coming to rest
low over fields
heavy
with harvest.

Ann Bonner

SOMEBODY

Somebody being a nobody,
Thinking to look like a somebody,
Said that he thought me a nobody:
Good little somebody-nobody,
Had you not known me a somebody,
Would you have called me a nobody?

Alfred, Lord Tennyson

RIDDLE

I have seas with no water,
coasts with no sand;
towns but no people,
mountains, no land.

Judith Nicholls

Answer on page 92.

RIDDLE

I have notes but no paper,
flats but no home;
hammers, no tool box,
no words but a song.

Judith Nicholls

Answer on page 92.

A RIDDLE

We are invisible,
But we run your day.
We shape what you do,
And what you say.
We're often broken,
But always the same.
And we can stop anything
Just with our name.
In one way we're nowhere,
But we're all around.
We can be made,
Remembered, or found.
Much is against us
Because we are there;
But that's why we're needed,
Although we don't care.
We're in your classrooms,
In playgrounds, *all* schools.
What are we, children?
You know us. We're . . .

Tony Bradman

Answer on page 92.

GOBBLEDESPOOK

Can you read this message?
The bottom of each letter
was bitten off and gobbled
by a ghost who knew no better.

Gina Douthwaite

WHAT'S IT?

Yesterday I made it,
today I wasted it.
My brother beat it
but I couldn't stand the noise.

Tomorrow I'll keep it;
the other day I lost it,
killing it in the playground,
talking to the boys.

Ian McMillan

Answer on page 92.

MORE RIDDLES

1

I am one of an endless family,
My brothers and sisters
Never far behind.
I crash and swirl,
Grind pebbles, growl,
And gnaw the bones of the land
Like a great wet dog.

2

I am a see-through pear
Hanging from my treeless branch.
A bit of a conjuror, I can ripen suddenly,
Or disappear at the touch of a switch.
Like the apple I am good for you
Lengthening your days.

3

I am at your beginning and your end.
I dog your footsteps
And cannot be shaken off.
Though I fade from view
You are never alone.
So silent that you often forget me,
I am still there,
Your constant dark spy and companion.

John Cotton

Answers on page 92.

MY PET

My
Pet
Doesn't
Have
A
Tail
My
Pet's
Got
No
Legs
My
Pet
Doesn't
Fly
Or
Sing
My
Pet
Doesn't
Beg

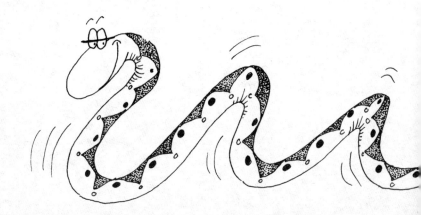

My
Pet
Isn't
Furry
But
It's
One
You
Won't
Mistake
For
My
Pet
Is
A
Curly
Wurly
Hissy
Kissy
Long
And
Lovely . . .

Tony Bradman

RIDDLE

Squishy and squashy
Sometimes like toffee.
Stretched long and tall
Or rolled up in a ball.
Pummelled and pounded
Until it is rounded
Blown up full of air
It makes them all stare
Then it goes pop
And you have to stop.
There is a real mess.
Can you make a guess?
   What it is?

Margaret Blount

Answer on page 92.

RIDDLES

1
Can you make a witch itch?

Take away her W
then she'll cease to trouble you.

2
Eat those sweeties if you dare;
you'll end up in the . . .

Marian Swinger

Answer on page 92.

RIDDLE ME WRONG

My first is in scare but not in fright
My second in spooky, no, that's not right.

My third is in riddle but not in ree
My fourth's in the fog and I'm all at sea.

I can't find my fifth, just lost my first
Of all the puzzles this seems the worst.

I'll make a new start, a brand new riddle
Lose the whole thread, get stuck in the middle.

My first has gone bonkers, my second's gone West
Forget the whole business, that'll be best.

David Harmer

DO YOU KNOW MY TEACHER?

She's got a piercing stare
and long black . . .

    (a) moustache
    (b) hair
    (c) teeth
    (d) shoes

She eats chips and beef
and has short sharp . . .

    (a) nails
    (b) fangs
    (c) doorstoppers
    (d) teef

She is slinky and thin
and has a pointed . . .

    (a) banana
    (b) chin
    (c) beard
    (d) umbrella

She has a long straight nose
and hairy little . . .

    (a) kneecaps
    (b) ears
    (c) children
    (d) toes

She has sparkling eyes
and wears school . . .

    (a) dinners
    (b) trousers
    (c) ties
    (d) buses

She comes from down south
and has a very big . . .

    (a) vocabulary
    (b) handbag
    (c) bottom
    (d) mouth

She yells like a preacher
yes, that's my . . .

    (a) budgie
    (b) stick
    (c) padlock
    (d) teacher!

John Rice

SIX ANSWERS ON A POSTCARD

1. Every Wednesday at 4.10 a.m.
2. It's best to trim them and wash them.

3. A hamster in a blue cage.
4. At the very bottom of the last page.

5. I found it about ten miles from the North Pole.
6. It's a type of water vole.

Martyn Wiley and Ian McMillan

Now make up some questions to go with these answers.
Keep your questions to one line, and make them
rhyme if you want – like our answers do.

1.
2.

3.
4.

5.
6.

A CHANCE IN FRANCE

'Stay at home,'
Mum said,

But I –
took a chance
in France,
turned grey
for the day
in St Tropez,
I forgot
what I did
in Madrid,
had some tussles
in Brussels
with a trio
from Rio,
lost my way
in Bombay,
nothing wrong
in Hong Kong,
felt calmer
in Palma,
and quite nice
in Nice,
yes, felt finer
in China,
took a room
in Khartoum
and a villa
in Manilla,

had a 'do'
in Peru
with a Llama
from Lima,
took a walk
in New York
with a man
from Milan,
lost a sneaker
in Costa Rica,
got lumbago
in Tobago,
felt a menace
in Venice,
was a bore
in Singapore,
lost an ear
in Korea
some weight
in Kuwait,
tried my best
as a guest
in old Bucharest,
got the fleas
in Belize
and came home.

Pie Corbett

DON'T BE SUCH A FUSSPOT

Don't be such a fusspot,
an always-in-a-rushpot.

Don't be such a weepypot
a sneak-to-mum-and-be-creepypot.

Don't be such a muddlepot,
a double-dose-of-troublepot.

Don't be such a wigglepot,
a sit-on-your-seat-don't-squigglepot.

Don't be such a muckypot,
a pick-up-slugs-and-be-yuckypot.

Don't be such a sleepypot,
a beneath-the-bedclothes-peepypot.

Don't be such a fiddlepot,
a mess-about-and-meddlepot.

Don't be such a bossypot,
a saucypot, a gigglepot,
Don't be such a lazypot,
a nigglepot, a slackpot.

And don't call *me* a crackpot . . .
Who do you think you are?

Brian Moses

IFFY BUTTY

Iffy Butty never knew,
Whether not, or whether to,
Whether yes, or whether no,
Whether stop, or whether go,
Whether here, or whether there,
Whether daren't, or whether dare,
Whether laugh, or whether cry,
Whether truth, or whether lie,
Whether bottom, or whether top,
Should I go on, or should I stop?

Vyanne Samuels

A Poem on the Neck of a Running Giraffe

PLEASE
DO NOT
MAKE F
UN OF
ME AN
D PLEAS
E DON'T
LAUGH
IT ISN'T
EASY T
O WRIT
E A PO
EM ON
THE NE
CK OF
A RUN
NING
GIRA
FFE.

Shel Silverstein

A POEM ABOUT A WOLF MAYBE TWO WOLVES

y
 o
  w
   e
    e
     e
      e
       e
        e
         e
          e
           e
            e
             e
              e
               e
                e

he comes running
across the field where
he comes running

                e
               e
              e
             e
            e
           e
          e
         e
        e
       e
      e
     e
    e
   e
  e
 e
e
 e
  e
   e

                    he comes running
                    across the field where
                    he comes running

y
 o
  w
   e
    e
     e
      e
       e
        e
         e
          e
           e
            e
             e
              e
               e
                e
                 e

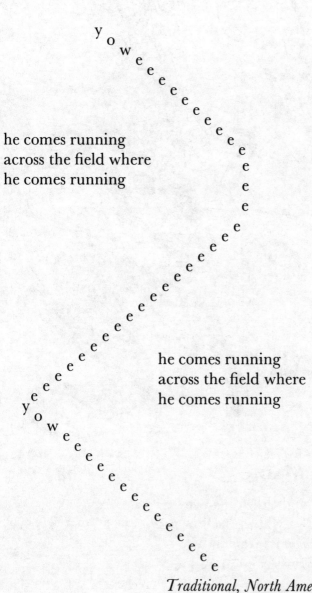

Traditional, North American Indian

ANIMAL MAGIC

Driving at night the *cat*'s-eyes
wink se*duc*tively at my yellow *beetle*
the road *snakes* its way
around the Sussex countryside
the words echo in my head as I drive

'Remember' she said 'I'm de*penguin* on you
so *donkey* me waiting'
and with a fond kiss we parted
it was a sorry *stoat* of affairs
'I love you an *ocelot* and no *mouse*take'
I yelled 'I'll *pig* you up at *ape*
even in the *reindeer*'
Sow here I am
Speeding home *duck*ing at low bridges
*rabbit*ing on to myself
Could she have been *lion* to me?
Is she just after my *doe*?
Will our love be heat *seal*ed or forever *colt*?
Am I really too *gull-a-bull*?
Is she being just plain *hawk*ward?
Maybe she is in love with someone else, the *cheetah*
Suddenly my eyes catch sight of something
that makes my *hare* stand on end
up a*herd* two nightshift policemen
worm into their *zebra* 3 *panda* car
*hound*ing some *teddy* boys
who've been *jay*walking on a *pelican* crossing
near the *Alsatian* Wide Building Society offices
which as *ewe* know is opposite
the multi-storey *shark* park just near the
*sheep*yard and *dog*s
The policemen are not *sheep*ish
in arresting the cola-*koala* swigging rascals
puffin and panting they put up little struggle
so the coppers set about *dragon* them off
to the station
it's plain to see that their *horse*play will cost them *deer*

John Rice

83

FOREST FUNGI

King Alfred's cakes
in calico wood,
bear's ears on the elder,
lemon peel
in the hollow oak
spread with witches' butter,

candle snuff and coral spot,
orange cap,
roof nails,
deadmens' fingers on
a fallen log,
white destroying angels,

wood hedgehogs
in the littered leaves,
sulphur tuft, stinkhorn;
fungi feeds
upon the forest
in the rotting rain.

Irene Rawnsley

This poem mentions 14 different kinds of fungi. Can
you find them all?

SWAP? SELL? SMALL ADS SELL FAST

1950 Dad. Good runner; needs one or
Two repairs; a few grey hairs but
Nothing a respray couldn't fix.
Would like a 1966 five speed turbo
In exchange: something in the sporty
Twin-carb range.

1920s Granny. Not many like this.
In such clean and rust free state.
You must stop by to view! All chrome
As new, original fascia retained
Upholstery unstained. Passed MOT
Last week: will only swap for some-
Thing quite unique.

1992 low mileage Brother. As eco-
Nomical as any other. Must mention
Does need some attention. Stream-
Lined, rear spoiler. Runs on milk
Baby oil and gripe water. Serviced;
Needs rear wash/wipe. Only one
Owner; not yet run in. Will swap
For anything.

Trevor Millum

NUTS

Olive Fig's a *gooseberry*,
she's *cherry melon*choly,
her *date* has *bean* and let her down –
he ran off with a *cauli*.

Flowers could not ap*pease* her
No, *Olive* took the *pip*,
'Such *chicory*! I am *appled*
that he should not *turnip*.'

Her *passion* it waned *parsley*
when some*yam* else did *sprout*,
'You're looking *radish*ing tonight.
Floret him. Let's go out.'

She's heard upon the *grape-lime*
this *mango*'s wild for her . . .
if *currant orange*ments bear *fruit*
these two won't stay a *pear*.

Gina Douthwaite

WEATHER WHEEL

(Start at any point and work clockwise)

WINTER WIND

frost blackens   seeds scatter

seeds form   earth kisses

flowers fade   snow blankets

AUTUMN CLOUD   ## SPRING RAIN

flowers open   roots tunnel

leaves stretch   seedlings sprout

buds thicken   stems unwind

SUMMER SUN

Moira Andrew

A SKIPPING ALPHABET

Hey!   bee
sea   dee
    eee
    eff
    gee
aitch   eye
jay   kay
    ell
    emm
    enn
    oh!
    pee
queue   are
ess   tea
    you
    vee

  double-you
     ex
    why?
    ZED
    and

    OUT

Wes Magee

ANSWERS

INDEX OF AUTHORS

ACKNOWLEDGEMENTS

The editor and publishers would like to thank the following for their kind permission to reprint copyright material in this book:

Moira Andrew for 'Weather Wheel', copyright © 1992 Moira Andrew, first published in *Schools Poetry Review* (1992); Margaret Blount for 'Riddle', copyright © 1993 Margaret Blount; Ann Bonner for 'A Riddle in the Dark' and 'It's a . . .', both copyright © 1993 Ann Bonner; Tony Bradman for 'A Riddle' and 'My Pet', both copyright © 1993 Tony Bradman; Dave Calder for 'Where?', copyright © 1992 Dave Calder; Pie Corbett for 'A Chance in France', copyright © 1993 Pie Corbett; John Cotton for 'Numbers', copyright © 1993 John Cotton, and 'Nature's Numbers', copyright © 1989 John Cotton, from *The Poetry File* (Nelson, 1989), 'More Riddles' copyright © John Cotton, from *The Biggest Riddle in the World*, with Fred Sedgwick (Mary Glasgow Publications, 1990); Viking Kestrel for 'Open/Close/Open/Close' by June Crebbin from *The Jungle Sale*. Copyright © 1988 June Crebbin, first published by Viking Kestrel 1988; Jennifer and Graeme Curry for 'Lotus Flower Takeaway', copyright © 1988 Jennifer and Graeme Curry from *Down Our Street* by Jennifer and Graeme Curry (Methuen, 1988); Gina Douthwaite for 'Gobbledespook' and 'Nuts', copyright © 1993 Gina Douthwaite; John Foster for 'Wordswords', copyright © 1993 John Foster, 'Says of the Week' copyright © 1993 John Foster, 'Tall Story' copyright © 1993 John Foster, all included by permission of the author; David Harmer for 'Riddle Me Wrong', copyright © 1993 David Harmer; Maggie Holmes for 'People Who . . .', copyright © 1992 Maggie Holmes; John Kitching for 'My First Is In' and 'A Bit of a Problem', both copyright © 1993 John Kitching; Cambridge University Press for 'An A–Z of Items Found on the School Roof . . .' and 'A Skipping Alphabet' both by Wes Magee and from *The Witch's Brew* (Cambridge University Press, 1989) and Wes Magee for 'An A–Z of Space Beasts', copyright © 1993 Wes Magee; Ray Mather for 'Ordering Words', copyright © 1989 Ray Mather from *Another Fourth Poetry Book* (Oxford University Press, 1989); Gerda Mayer for 'A Good Spell for Sarah', copyright © 1993 Gerda Mayer; Ian McMillan for 'What's It?' and 'Coded Nursery Rhymes', copyright © 1993 Ian McMillan; Ian McMillan and Martyn Wiley for 'My Model Aeroplane' and 'Six Answers on a Postcard', copyright © 1993 Martyn Wiley and Ian McMillan; Trevor Millum for 'Ten Little Schoolchildren' and 'Swap? Sell? Small Ads Sell Fast', both copyright © 1988 Trevor Millum and from *Warning – Too Much Schooling Can Damage Your Health*

(Nelson, 1988); Carcanet Press Ltd for 'The Loch Ness Monster's Song' by Edwin Morgan from *Collected Poems* (Carcanet, 1990); Brian Moses for 'Sounds' and 'Don't Be Such a Fusspot', copyright © 1993 Brian Moses; Faber and Faber Ltd for 'Lines' by Judith Nicholls from *Magic Mirror and Other Poems*, and 'Riddle: I Have Seas With No Water' and 'Riddle: I Have Notes but No Paper' both by Judith Nicholls and from *Dragonsfire and Other Poems* (Faber and Faber); Irene Rawnsley for 'On the Lawn One Morning', copyright © 1989 Irene Rawnsley, and 'Forest Fungi', copyright © 1993 Irene Rawnsley, both reprinted by permission of the author; John Rice for 'The Cat Sat on the Mat', 'Mr Body, the Head' and 'Animal Magic', copyright © 1993 John Rice, 'A Listen to This', copyright © 1991 John Rice from *Toughie Toffee* (Fontana Lions) and 'Do You Know My Teacher?' copyright © 1989 John Rice from *Read a Poem, Write a Poem* (Blackwell Publishers); Methuen Childen's Books for 'Obeah One' and 'Iffy Butty' by Vyanne Samuels from *Beams* (Methuen Children's Books); Edite Kroll Literary Agency for 'A Poem on the Neck of a Running Giraffe' from *Where the Sidewalk Ends* by Shel Silverstein, copyright © 1974 by Evil Eye Music, Inc., and 'Poemsicle' from *A Light in the Attic* by Shel Silverstein, copyright © 1981 by Evil Eye Music, Inc., both poems by permission of Edite Kroll Literary Agency; Matt Simpson for 'Alphabetics', copyright © 1993 Matt Simpson and 'Think of a Number', copyright © 1992 Matt Simpson from *The Pigs' Thermal Underwear – Poems for Children* (Headland, 1992); Ian Souter for 'The Fortunate Boy' and 'Word Maths', copyright © 1993 Ian Souter; Roger Stevens for 'Haiku', copyright © 1993 Roger Stevens; Marian Swinger for 'Riddles' and 'Can You Make a Witch Itch', copyright © 1993 Marian Swinger; Charles Thomson for 'Demolition Dan' and 'Counting Horrors', copyright © 1993 Charles Thomson; Barrie Wade for 'Studup', copyright © 1991 Barrie Wade, from *Barley Barley* (Oxford University Press, 1991) and Oxford University Press for 'Code Shoulder', copyright © Barrie Wade 1989. Reprinted from *Conkers* by Barrie Wade (1989) by permission of Oxford University Press; Clive Webster for 'Acrostic', copyright © 1993 Clive Webster; Bernard Young for 'ABQ' and 'Three Notes Concerning a Squashed Bee', both copyright © 1991 Bernard Young; Benjamin Zephaniah for 'According to My Mood' from *You'll Love This Stuff* (Cambridge University Press).

Every effort has been made to trace the copyright holders, but the editor and publishers apologize if any inadvertent omission has been made.